First published 1983

L&S PUBLISHING

(A Division of Syme Media Pty Ltd)

99 Argus Street, Cheltenham 3192, Australia

The author, photographer and publisher thank:
Malcolm Brownlee, Melbourne
Diane and Jida Gulpilil, Melbourne
Jim Howes, Melbourne
John Mundene, Ramingining
Dr. Nicholas Peterson, Canberra
Robyn Redlich, Melbourne
Tom Treasure, Ramingining
and the children of Ramingining School
for their help in preparing this book

Book design by John Van Loon and Neil McLeod
Set in 18 pt Cloister by Dovatype, Melbourne
Printed by Tien Wah Press, Singapore

National Library of Australia
Cataloguing-in-Publication data:

Gulpilil.
   The birirrk.

For children.
ISBN 0 86898 061 7.

(1). Aborigines, Australian – Legends. I. McLeod,
Neil. II. Title.

389.2'049915

The Birirrk
OUR ANCESTORS OF THE DREAMING

Told by
Gulpilil

Photographs by
Neil McLeod

Published by
L&S Publishing
for Gordon & Gotch Limited

Long long time before our Dreaming, the
earth at our feet had no shape, it had no
colour, there was no light, and nothing
walked across it.
There were no emu tracks and no kangaroo
tracks. It was dust without water, no river
flowed, the earth was empty.

Into the darkness came the Birirrk. They came from far away and made their tracks on the ground. The Birirrk were our great spirit ancestors. Their tracks across the earth made the Dreaming paths and painted it with light and shadows.

The Birirrk could enter the rock. They blew on its face and the rocks opened to let them inside. This was how they came out and returned when there was danger. When the wind blew strongly the Birirrk ran back to the rocks for safety. Their thin bodies would break in the strong wind.

Out of the dust they shaped our mountains and over the land they made the great rivers. When that was done, the Birirrk made the shapes of the animals to live in them. With the water, came grass and trees, and the animals to eat the grass, to shelter beneath the trees and to drink at the river.

They showed their children, our ancestors, the spirit in the water. They taught us how to drink the spirit of the earth, our Mother. 'Drink the water,' said the Birirrk, 'it is the spirit.'

We entered the rivers and they were all around us. The water played with us. The Birirrk told us, 'Listen to its story. It is a Dreaming story.' We listened and knew it was a Dreaming place. We kept its story.

The Birirrk made the shapes of water lilies and the yams. They showed their children, our people, how to find and eat yams and said, 'These are yams. Yams are also men.'

In the face of the waters are the plants that also drink it. The water is in the canoe trees and in the lily bulbs we eat. It is the spirit of the Birirrk. It is also in the fish that are in it.

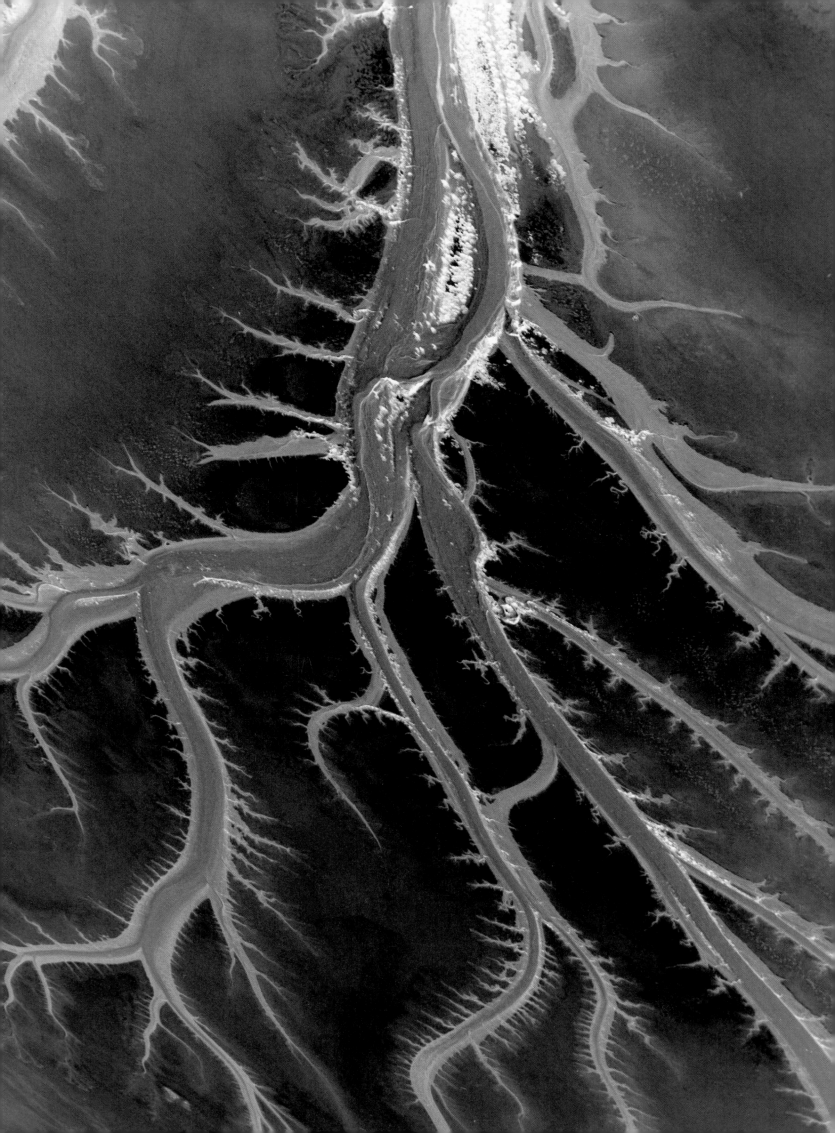

The Birirrk walked across the earth, and made the great Dreaming tracks. Here they made waterholes where our people drink. There they made the rocks where our people shelter when they are hunting. They came to rest and put themselves on rock. 'This will be a Dreaming place,' they said.

When all this was done, the great ancestors taught their children, our people, about the shape of the kangaroo. They taught us where the water slept beneath the earth and how to know the Dreaming places.

The Birirrk were great hunters. They used
the wind to hide their coming from the
kangaroo. In the shadows of the trees our
ancestors were like shadows.
They made the boomerang and the spear
and said, 'These will kill the kangaroo.
Kangaroo are also men.'

As the light filled the sky, the Birirrk made
the shapes of the birds and taught them how
to fly.
'These are also men,' they told us.

On the earth, the Birirrk said, 'Look at the colours.' They showed us the red that came from the blood of their fighting and hunting, the sacred white pipe clay that is kept by a giant kangaroo, the yellow that marks the cliffs of our land and is the sacred colour of the Yirritja, and the black that they made with the great fire they used to shape us.

They showed us the charcoal from the fires of their great Dreaming tracks and told us, 'With these colours you can keep the Dreaming.'

The Birirrk told us, 'Put the Dreaming on rocks and there will be food and children. These will be Dreaming places. In these places you can sing and the spirit will hear you. You can dance and the spirit will see you. You can tell the story to your young men and they will know the Dreaming.'

The Birirrk told our women how to have
their children. The children play the games
they taught them. They sometimes pretend
to sneak up and kill a man or a kangaroo.
The boys go out to learn how to spear fish
and the girls go out to bring home bush
food.

They play at being grown men and women.
They make bark houses the same as their
parents, and the girls lie beside the boys as
wives and husbands. Then they are
embarrassed. They laugh and run away.

'We will leave soon, but we will return at
the Dreaming places through your songs
and dances, your painting and your telling.
You will know us as we come from the rocks
and the earth at these times.'

To make fire, the Birirrk took the stick between their hands and rubbed quickly. The smoke rose towards the sky. They put some grass in their hands and made it smoke. Then they gently blew on it and put the fire in the grass.

They showed us how to cook the kangaroo, our food, and said, 'You will always need fire. Keep it in these sticks.'

The Birirrk vanished. They became the
waterholes, the hills, the rivers and the rocks
of the earth, our Mother. They left us the
stories of how to hunt the emu, kangaroo
and goanna.

They left the stories of making the canoe
and of teaching our children. These stories
are in the earth. They are the laws that are
ours to keep and to keep us.

The Birirrk, our ancestors, are in the earth,
our Mother. They are in us and in our
children at the Dreaming places. The earth,
our Mother, is in us from these places.
These rocks and hills, these rivers and
waterholes, are our great ancestors.
They are the Birirrk, our spirit.

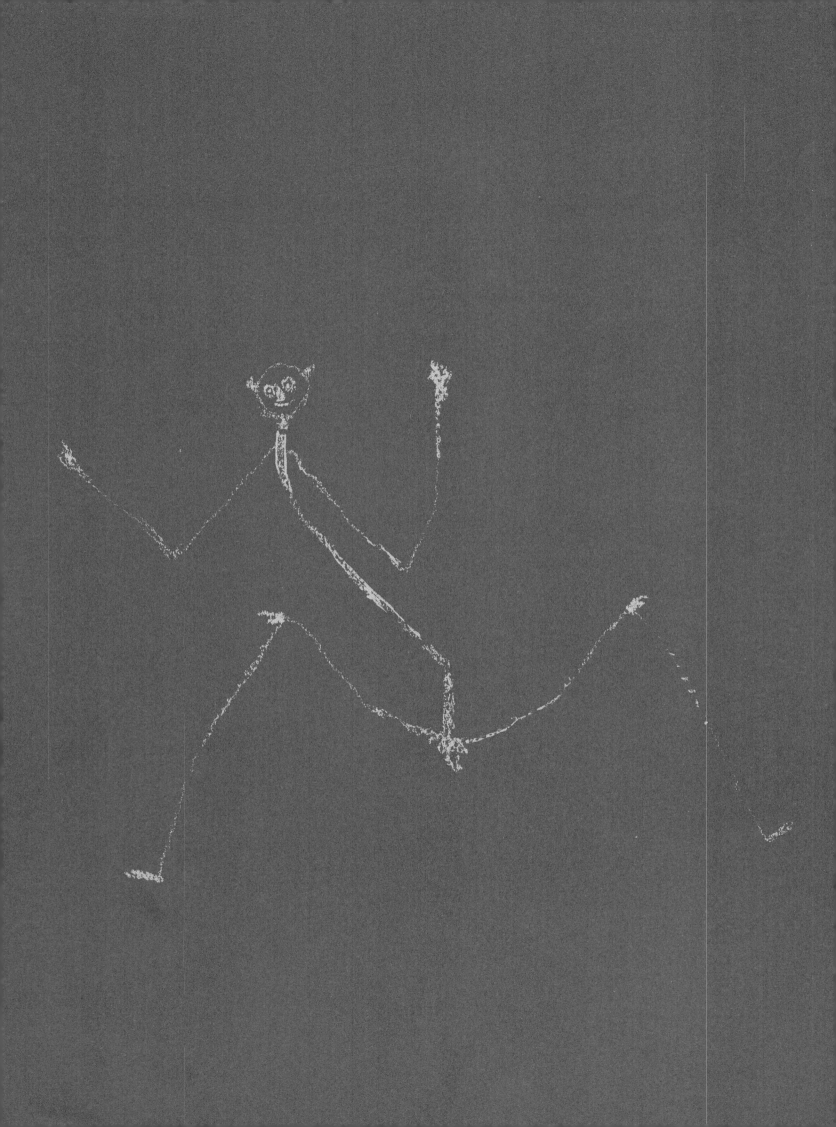